The Wildlife Trusts Guide to

BUTTERFLIES AND MOTHS

The Wildlife Trusts Guide to

BUTTERFLIES
AND MOTHS

Series Editor Nicholas Hammond

Illustrated by Stuart Carter

NEW HOLLAND

First published in 2002 by
New Holland Publishers (UK) Ltd
Garfield House
86-88 Edgware Road
London W2 2EA
www.newhollandpublishers.com

10 9 8 7 6 5 4 3 2

This edition published in 2002 by
Advanced Marketing (UK) Ltd, Bicester, Oxfordshire

ISBN 1 84330 244 6

Publishing Manager: Jo Hemmings
Project Editor: Mike Unwin
Production: Joan Woodroffe

Packaged by Wildlife Art Ltd:
www.wildlife-art.co.uk
Design and Cover Design: Sarah Crouch
Art/Copy editor: Sarah Whittley
Proof-reading and Index: Rachel Lockwood
Illustrator: Stuart Carter

Reproduction by Modern Age
Repro Co. Ltd, Hong Kong
Printed and bound in Singapore by
Kyodo Printing Co (Singapore) Pte Ltd

Contents

Since 1912, The Wildlife Trusts have been speaking out for
wildlife and undertaking practical action at the local level
throughout the UK. Believing that wildlife is essential to a
healthy environment for all, The Wildlife Trusts work with
people from all walks of life – communities, industry,
government, landowners, and families – to make sure nature
gets a chance amongst all of the pressures of the
modern world.

With years of experience and the service of the UK's top
naturalists, The Wildlife Trusts and Wildlife Watch – the UK's
leading club for young environmentalists – play a key part in
restoring the balance between new developments and the
natural world. With the specialist skills of volunteers and staff
they manage more than 2,300 wildlife reserves (totalling more
than 80,000 hectares), which are among the
finest sites in the UK.

Their members, who number more than 340,000, contribute
to their achievements by their generosity and hard work, and
by spreading the message to everyone that wildlife matters.

The Wildlife Trusts is a registered charity (number 207238).
For membership, and other details, please phone
The Wildlife Trusts on 0870 0367711 or log on to
www.wildlifetrusts.org

Butterflies are the most obvious of insects and, probably with the exception of the "cabbage whites", the most popular. They are seen during the day, mostly in the warmer months from spring through summer to autumn. Many moths are nocturnal and usually seen when they enter the house or come to a lighted window. There are, however, some day-flying species that are so colourful people think they are butterflies.

Moths and butterflies are both seen seasonally. A common garden butterfly is the peacock, especially if there is a bed of nettles on which the caterpillars might feed. The first peacocks are seen as the weather warms in March and they emerge from hibernation to breed. After May they seem to disappear, this is because the adults have bred and the new generation are developing from eggs to larvae to pupae, emerging as butterflies from July to September. On sunny autumn days they will be seen feeding on the nectar or juices of rotting windfall fruit, before hibernating throughout the winter. You might come across one in a corner of the garden shed or even in the house. The life cycle of all insects includes a number of stages. These stages vary between species in terms of the timing, but each cycle is timed to provide the maximum opportunity for the larvae to feed.

Butterflies and moths belong to a huge order of insects, known as Lepidoptera, which has over 165,000 species worldwide, with 2300 in the British Isles. Moths are much more numerous and of the British species of Lepidoptera about 70 are butterflies. Butterflies and moths are distinguished from other insects by being densely covered with tiny, powdery scales ("Lepidoptera" is derived from the Greek "scaly wings"). Sizes vary from being so tiny that a magnifying glass is needed to see them to some tropical species that are the size of small birds.

Butterflies and moths have bodies that are in three parts: the head carries the eyes, antennae and mouth-parts; the thorax has three segments, the first of which carries the front legs, the second of which carries the forewings and the middle pair of legs, and the third of which carries the hindwings and the third pair of legs; the third segment of the body is the abdomen, which has no legs, but does have sexual and digestive functions. Butterflies can be distinguished from moths by their clubbed or knobbed antennae. At rest butterflies tend to hold their wings vertically above the body.

Vision is through two large compound eyes and a pair of ocelli, or simple eyes. The antennae are found between the eyes. They are complex sense organs that can pick up chemical and tactile messages. Butterflies have antennae that are more uniform than moths', which are very varied.

The vast majority of moths and butterflies feed on nectar and other liquids. They lack jaws, which have evolved into tongues. The tongue or proboscis is long and slender enough to probe flowers. When not in use the proboscis is coiled up and cannot be seen.

The wings of moths and butterflies may be quite strikingly coloured and patterned, but they may also demonstrate protective colouring. The bright metallic colours, particularly purples and blues, are due to the structure of the scales and if they are damaged the colours will fade. The bright colours must play a role in communication between individuals. Males have specialised scent glands in the wings. The pheromones that are produced help to attract females over a distance and also help to differentiate between the sexes of species in which males and females look alike.

Wings of some species may have roughly circular markings that look like eyes. It is thought that these distract predatory birds from the body of the insect. It may survive if a bird pecks a chunk of the wing, whereas a peck to the body will almost inevitably be fatal. It is not uncommon to see butterflies such as the small tortoiseshell with a triangular "bird-tear" in its wing. Another protective mechanism employed by moths is flash colouring, where the forewings are well camouflaged, but the underwing is brightly coloured. When the moth is disturbed the bright yellow of the large yellow underwing will confuse a bird, because the moment the moth comes to rest the yellow disappears. Butterflies may have brightly coloured wings, but the underside, which is the area visible when the insect is at rest, may be very well camouflaged so that the resting animal looks like a dead leaf.

Wings help to warm butterflies to the temperature that they need to fly. Their bodies need to reach about 30°C before they can take off. The dark-coloured areas of the wings absorb the most heat, even on cool days when there is some sunshine.

To achieve this temperature they sunbathe with their wings open. Nocturnal moths reach the required body temperature by shivering the wings.

All butterflies and moths pass through four very different stages, during which they metamorphose completely. The first stage is an egg. The female lays an egg, in most cases on the plant on which the caterpillar will feed. Eggs are tiny and usually overlooked by the human eye. From the eggs hatch the larvae or caterpillars. These look nothing like the adult insect. They are worm-like with biting jaws and in addition to the three pairs of legs on the thorax have stumpy legs on the abdomen. Caterpillar's moult four or five times during their life. Before the final moult the caterpillar which has become large and fat seeks a place of safety, often burrowing beneath the soil, or protected within a silken cocoon that the larva spins, or hanging from its food plant. This final moult is the metamorphosis between caterpillar and chrysalis or pupa. The pupa has a harder outer skin than the larva and barely moves at all. However, inside, its tissues liquefy and it develops into the adult insect. The time for this remarkable change to happen varies. In some species in warm weather it may be as short as a week, while in many it may take two or three weeks and in some it may be several months, because it is in this stage that the species spends the winter.

The longevity of butterflies and moths vary between species and between broods. Many species produce one brood a year, but others may produce more. The first butterfly to appear in early spring is the brimstone, which hibernates as an adult. Males emerge first and can be seen patrolling their territories. The greenish white female appears a couple of weeks later. Eggs are laid in May and June, the larvae are seen in June and July and the adults emerge in August. Sometimes among double-brooded species, some of the second brood will reach adulthood before winter and hibernate, while others will spend the winter as larvae or pupae.

The 127 species in this book give an introduction to the fascinating variety of butterflies and moths, but are a tiny portion of the European species and a miniscule representation of the world's 165,000. Enjoy their beauty.

Apollo
Parnassius apollo

SIZE AND DESCRIPTION Forewing is 35–42 mm. Upperside is white dusted with grey with large black spots on forewing and red eyespots on hindwing. Sexes are similar, but female has greyer upperside. There are many different races with slightly different markings. Antennae are grey. Larvae are dark brown to black with orange spots and tufts.

HABITAT Occurs in mountainous areas of southern and central Europe up to 1800 m. Rather lower levels in northern Europe.

FOOD/HABITS Flies in July and August. Larvae eat stonecrops.

Scarce swallow tail
Iphiclides podalirius
SIZE AND DESCRIPTION Forewing is 32–40 mm in male. Female is a little larger. Sexes are similar, very pale, creamy yellow with black markings, six stripes on upper forewing. Larva looks like green slug with faint yellow stripes.
HABITAT Often occurs in fruit orchards up to 1800 m. Found in southern and eastern Europe. Vagrants occasionally turn up in British Isles.
FOOD/HABITS Flies in March to September – may have generations.
Larvae feed on blackthorn and also on fruit trees.

Swallowtail
Papilio machaon
SIZE AND DESCRIPTION
Forewing is 32–38 mm. Male and female are similar. Uppersides yellow with black markings, red eyespot at corner of hindwings, black band dusted with blue. Larvae are large and green, striped black with red spots.
HABITAT Meadows and banks with wild flowers, especially umbellifers. Widespread in Europe, restricted to Norfolk in British Isles.
FOOD/HABITS Flies in April to May and July to August. Two or three generations in southern Europe. Larvae feed on umbellifers such as milk parsley, fennel and wild carrot.

Black-veined white
Aporia crataegi

SIZE AND DESCRIPTION Forewing is 28–34 mm. Upperside is white, grey at tip of forewing, with dark brown or black veins. Underside is similar with a few black scales.

Larvae are grey with dark backs and red-brown lines.

HABITAT Found in open country from sea level up to 1800 m. Widespread in southern and central Europe but became extinct in British Isles in 1920s.

FOOD/HABITS Flies in May to July. One generation a year. Larvae usually feed on hawthorn but also prunus.

Small white
Artogeia rapae

SIZE AND DESCRIPTION Forewing is 15–30 mm. Upperside is white, with one black or grey spot on male's forewing and two on female's. Black or grey forewing patches extend further along the leading edge than down the side of the wing. Two spots on underside of forewing in both sexes. Underside of hindwings is yellowish. The larva is green, with a yellow stripe running along its side.

HABITAT Gardens, hedges and flowery places across Europe. Abundant to the point of being a pest.

FOOD/HABITS Flies March to October. Two to four broods. Eggs are laid on leaves. Larvae feed on brassicae and nasturtiums.

Green-veined white
Artogeia napi
SIZE AND DESCRIPTION Forewing is 18–30 mm. Black spots and patches on the forewing are less distinct than in the small or large white. Grey lines along veins on underside of hindwings. Larva is similar to that of small white, without the yellow.
HABITAT Gardens, hedges, woodland margins and other flowery places throughout Europe.
FOOD/HABITS Flies March to November. Larvae eat crucifers, such as garlic mustard, lady's smock and watercress.

Large white
Pieris brassicae
SIZE AND DESCRIPTION
Forewing is 25–35 mm. Black tips extend halfway down the forewing's edge. Upperside of forewing has two black spots in female, one in male.
Underside of forewing has two spots in both sexes. Caterpillar is green, with black spots and yellow stripes.

HABITAT Gardens and other flowery places.
FOOD/HABITS Flies April to October. Eggs are laid on the underside of leaves. The larvae feed on brassicae and nasturtiums.

Bath white
Pontia daplidice

SIZE AND DESCRIPTION Forewing is 21–24 mm. Upperside is white with dark grey/black markings to tip of forewing, hindwing is greyer. Underside has grey-green markings. Female has larger markings on forewing and dark spot on underside of forewing. Larva is greenish, with three yellow stripes.

HABITAT Found in lowland up to 1800 m, on rough ground and meadows. Occurs in southern and central Europe, rare vagrant to British Isles.

FOOD/HABITS Flies in February and March onwards. Migratory. May have two or more generations. Larvae feed on mignonette and mustard plants.

Orange tip
Anthocaris cardamines

SIZE AND DESCRIPTION Forewing is 20–25 mm. Male has orange wing-tips and green-blotches on underside of hindwing. Female has greyish patches on forewing, and mottled underwings.

HABITAT Hedgerows, gardens, damp meadows and woodland margins. All Europe, except south-west or east Spain or northern Scandinavia.

FOOD/HABITS Flies April to June. Larvae eat garlic mustard, lady's smock, but also sweet rocket and honesty in gardens. Overwinters as a pupa.

Brimstone
Gonepteryx rhamni

SIZE AND DESCRIPTION Forewing is 25–30 mm. Male's wings are
sulphur yellow on top, but paler beneath. Female is white, with
a pale green tinge, but she lacks the large white's black
markings. Larva is green, with white stripes along the side.
HABITAT Open woodland, gardens and flowery places. All
Europe, but not most of Scotland and northern Scandinavia.
FOOD/HABITS Flies February to September. Larvae eat buckthorn
and alder buckthorn. Adults overwinter in holly or ivy.

Clouded yellow
Colias crocea

SIZE AND DESCRIPTION Forewing is 23–27 mm. Upperside is strong orange yellow with black borders to both fore and hindwings. Female colouring is suffused with grey. Underside of both sexes has black spots on ground colour of dusky yellow-grey. Larva is green with pale stripe.

HABITAT Found on heaths and open areas up to 1800 m, in southern and central Europe. Migrates to Britain.

FOOD/HABITS Flies in April and May onwards. Several generations a year. Larvae feed on clover and vetches.

Lesser clouded yellow
Colias hyale

SIZE AND DESCRIPTION
Forewing is 21–25 mm. Male has pale yellow upperwing with dark grey or black borders fringed with red. Female is white, tinged with yellow-green. Larva is green and speckled black with a white stripe along each side.

HABITAT Found in flower meadows and fields up to and above 1800 m, in southern and eastern Europe. Absent in Italy. Migrates north.

FOOD/HABITS Has two generations, which fly in May to June and August to September. The larvae eat lucerne and vetches.

Brown hairstreak
Thecla betulae
SIZE AND DESCRIPTION Forewing is
17–20 mm. Upperside is brown with
orange patch on forewing. Female is larger
with bigger, brighter orange patch.
Underside orange-yellow with white lines.
Plump, green larvae.
HABITAT Found in woodland from low to
moderate heights. Occurs across central
Europe including southern Britain.
FOOD/HABITS Flies in July and August. Eggs laid on
twigs to hatch in the following spring. Larvae feed
on blackthorn and other prunus leaves and birch
and beech. One generation a year.

Purple hairstreak
Quercusia quercus
SIZE AND DESCRIPTION Forewing is
14–19 mm. Upperside is dark with
purplish-blue sheen and black margins.
Underside is grey with white line and pale
orange spots on hindwing corner. Larva is
reddish-brown with grey-brown line
down back.

HABITAT Found in woodlands up to 1500 m
throughout Europe including Britain but not in
northern Scandinavia.
FOOD/HABITS Flies in July and August. Larvae
feed on oak buds and leaves. One generation
per year. The eggs hatch in the following spring.

White-letter hairstreak
Strymonidia w-album
SIZE AND DESCRIPTION Forewing is 14–17 mm. Upperside is dark brown, sometimes with orange flush on forewing. Short tails to hindwing. Female slightly larger, not so dark brown. Larva is short and broad, yellow-green with dark green on middle of back.
HABITAT Found in woodland and trees up to 1300 m. Occurs from northern Spain to southern Scandinavia, UK and Turkey.
FOOD/HABITS Flies in July. Larvae feed on tree leaves such as lime, elm and wych elm. One generation a year. Eggs are laid in July and August to hatch in the following spring.

Green hairstreak
Callophrys rubi

SIZE AND DESCRIPTION Forewing is 13–15 mm. Upperside is brown or grey; underside is green. Eyespots have white borders. The female is similar. The larva is broad and plump. It is green with a dark line down central back.
HABITAT Found in heathland and moorland and rough ground, with heather or gorse. Occurs up to 2100 m, widespread and common throughout Europe.
FOOD/HABITS Flies in March. Larvae feed on bird's-foot trefoil, gorse, buckthorn, bramble. One generation a year. Pupae overwinter for adults to emerge in spring.

Small copper
Lycaena phlaeas
SIZE AND DESCRIPTION   Forewing is 10–17 mm. Bright forewing is like shiny copper, with dark flecks and brown edges. Caterpillar is small and green.
HABITAT   Gardens, flowery wasteland and heathland across Europe.
FOOD/HABITS   Flies February to November. Two or three broods, with adults from the third brood being rather small. Food plants for larvae are common sorrel, sheep's sorrel and docks.

Common blue
Polyommatus icarus
SIZE AND DESCRIPTION   Forewing is 14–18 mm. Upperside of male's wings are violet blue; the upperside of the female's wings are dark brown. Small greenish larva.
HABITAT   Flowery grasslands, roadsides, sand dunes and wasteland. Occurs throughout the whole of Europe.
FOOD/HABITS   Flies April to October. Two or three broods. Food consists of leguminous plants, particularly horseshoe vetch. Winters as a small larva.

Holly blue
Celastrina argiolus
SIZE AND DESCRIPTION Forewing is 12–18 mm.
Upperside of male is violet blue. Female is
paler blue, edged with a broad dark band. The
dark band is broader in the second brood.
Underside of the wings is pale blue-grey. The
caterpillar is small, green and slug-like. This is the
blue most likely to be seen in gardens.
HABITAT Woodland margins, hedgerows, parks and
gardens. Found across Europe, except in Scotland and
northern Scandinavia.
FOOD/HABITS Flies April to September. First brood
feeds on flowers and developing fruit of holly; second
brood feeds on ivy. Adults drink honeydew, sap and
juices of carrion. Winters as a pupa.

Silver-studded blue
Plebejus argus
SIZE AND DESCRIPTION Forewing is 12–15
mm. Upperside is deep blue with black
borders. Underside varies between shades
of grey, with black white-ringed spots on
forewing; hindwing has black spots with green
centres. Female is brown. Larva is green with dark
black/brown stripe with white borders.
HABITAT Found on grassy banks and heaths throughout Europe
except for northern England, northern Scandinavia, Ireland and
Mediterranean islands.
FOOD/HABITS Flies in May. Has two generations a year, but only one
in northern Europe. Lays eggs in summer and caterpillars hatch the
next spring. Larvae feed on bird's-foot trefoil, bilberry, ling and gorse.

Purple emperor
Apatura iris

SIZE AND DESCRIPTION Forewing is 31–37 mm. Upperside very dark, almost black, with iridescent blue flush, with white spots and stripe. Underside brown with white markings, orange eye spot on under forewing. Female is larger with larger white markings, lacks blue flush. Larva is green, with tiny white spots, with two horns on head and yellow stripes on oblique body.

HABITAT Found in woodland, in treetops, up to 900 m. Occurs in central Europe including south-east England.

FOOD/HABITS Flies in July and August. Larvae feed on willow trees, especially goat willow and grey sallow. One generation a year. Lays eggs in August, overwinters as caterpillar.

White admiral
Limenitis camilla

SIZE AND DESCRIPTION Forewing is 26–30 mm. Upperside dark with broken line of white spots on forewing, broad white line on hindwing. Underside is mottled brown and grey. The sexes are similar. Larva is green with two lines of brown tufts down back.

HABITAT Found in lowland woodland up to 900 m. Occurs in central Europe including southern England.

FOOD/HABITS Flies in June and July. Single generation a year. Larvae feed on honeysuckle and overwinter before pupating.

Painted lady
Cynthia cardui

SIZE AND DESCRIPTION Forewing is 20–25 mm. Upperside is orange, with a black forewing tip patched with white. Underside is pale, with three blue underwing spots. Black caterpillar has tufts of hairs and a yellow-and-red stripe.

HABITAT Flowery places, including roadsides and gardens. Across Europe, but is a migrant from North Africa. Does not survive European winter.

FOOD/HABITS Flies April to November, arriving in Britain in late spring/early summer. Two broods in Europe, but produces broods throughout the year in North Africa. Eats thistles and sometimes stinging nettles.

Red admiral
Vanessa atalanta

SIZE AND DESCRIPTION Forewing is 30 mm. Upperside is a velvety dark brown, with bright orange bars on each wing. Tips of forewings are black with white markings. Underside of hindwing is pale brown, while underside of forewing shows orange, blue and white markings. Dark caterpillar has bristles and a pale yellow stripe along the side.

HABITAT Flowery places across Europe. Absent from northern Scandinavia. Resident in southern Europe, moves north in spring.

FOOD/HABITS Flies May to October. There are two broods. Larvae feed on nettles. Adults feed on rotting fruit in autumn.

Small tortoiseshell
Aglais urticae
SIZE AND DESCRIPTION Forewing is 25 mm. Upperside is bright orange and black, with a row of blue spots on the trailing edge of the hindwings. Caterpillar is bristly and black.
HABITAT All kinds of flowery places. Common across the whole of Europe.
FOOD/HABITS Flies March to October. Adults overwinter, often in buildings. Larvae feed on nettles, elms and hops.

Large tortoiseshell
Nymphalis polychloros
SIZE AND DESCRIPTION Forewing is 25–32 mm. The sexes are similar. Upperside is orange-brown with dark markings, dark border on forewings, blue bordered dark near edge of hindwing. Underside is dark. Larva is dark with orange-brown spines.
HABITAT Found in lowland woodland up to 1500 m in southern and western Europe, including southern England. Migrates into southern Scandinavia. Absent from Ireland.
FOOD/HABITS Flies in June and July. Larvae feed on trees such as elm and willow, birch and poplar. Overwinters as adult.

Peacock
Inachis io
SIZE AND DESCRIPTION Forewing is 30 mm. Wings have four large, peacock-like "eyes". Upperside is orange, while underside is very dark brown. Caterpillar is black and bristly.
HABITAT Flowery places, including gardens. Across Europe, and as far north as southern Scandinavia.
FOOD/HABITS Flies March to May, and July to September. Larvae feed on nettles. Adults often overwinter in buildings.

Comma
Polygonia c-album

SIZE AND DESCRIPTION Forewing is 23 mm. Wings have jagged edges. Orange upperside, with black and buff markings. Underside of hindwing has a white comma-shaped mark. Caterpillar is black and sparsely bristled. Its rear end becomes white, making it look like a bird dropping.

HABITAT Woodland margins, gardens, hedges and other flowery places. Common across Europe, but absent from Ireland, northern Britain, and northern Scandinavia.

FOOD/HABITS Flies March to September. There are two broods. Second brood is darker. Overwinters, with adults hanging from leaves. Larvae feed on stinging nettles, hops and elms.

Dark green fritillary
Mesoacidalia aglaia

SIZE AND DESCRIPTION Forewing is 24–29 mm. Upperside is tawny brown with dark markings. Underside forewing is yellow-buff with dark markings, hindwing green-washed with white spots. Larva is very dark brown with rows of spiky black tufts. Female is similar but paler.

HABITAT Found in lowland meadows and heaths. Occurs throughout western Europe.

FOOD/HABITS Flies in June and July. Larvae feed on violets. Single generation a year. Overwinters as caterpillar. Pupates after spinning a tent within leaves.

Silver-washed fritillary
Argynnis paphia

SIZE AND DESCRIPTION Forewing is 27–35 mm. Upperside is tawny brown with black markings. Underside paler forewing, with green-washed hindwing. Female similar but duller. Larva is dark with spiky red-brown tufts.

HABITAT Found in lowland woodland clearings up to 1400 m. Occurs in southern and central Europe, including southern England and southern Scandinavia.

FOOD/HABITS Flies in June to August. Larvae feed mainly on dog-violet. Pupa is hung from foodplant. Overwinters as caterpillar.

Glanville fritillary
Melitaea cinxia

SIZE AND DESCRIPTION Forewing is 16–20 mm, but second brood is smaller. Upperside is tawny brown with dark patterning. Underside forewing orange with few dark markings, hindwing patterned orange, black and white. Larva is black with white spots and short black tufts.

HABITAT Found in lowland meadows up to 1800 m. Occurs in southern and central Europe but only in Isle of Wight in Britain.

FOOD/HABITS Flies in May and June, and August and September. Larvae feed on plantain. Overwinters as caterpillar.

Marbled white
Melanargia galathea

SIZE AND DESCRIPTION Forewing is 23–26 mm. Upperwing is
yellowish white with very heavy black markings. Underside is
paler, hindwing grey and white with small eyespots. Female is
larger and paler, with more extensive white. Larva is pale green
or pale brown with a yellow or white line along sides.
HABITAT Found in grassy areas up to 1500 m throughout
western Europe, including southern England.
FOOD/HABITS Flies in June and July. Larvae feed on grasses such
as cock's-foot. Overwinters as caterpillar.

Grayling
Hipparchia semele
SIZE AND DESCRIPTION
Forewing is 21–25 mm. Upperside brown washed with orange, with two small eyespots on forewing and one on hindwing. Underside has pale orange forewing with two eyespots and a mottled hindwing. Female is larger with more yellow on upperside. Larva is pale yellow-white with brown stripes.
HABITAT Found in heath and rough grassland with bare ground patches for basking in sunshine. Subspecies occur throughout central and southern Europe, more coastal in Great Britain.
FOOD/HABITS Flies in July and August. Larvae feed on grasses.

Gatekeeper
Pyronia tithonus
SIZE AND DESCRIPTION Forewing is 17–25 mm. Usually smaller than the meadow brown, with orange patches on the wings. "Eyes" are black with two highlights. Green or brown larva.
HABITAT Hedgerows and woodland margins. Southern Britain and Ireland, and south across the rest of Europe.
FOOD/HABITS Flies July to September. Larval food plants are fine-leaved grasses. Adults are fond of bramble blossom and marjoram.

Meadow brown
Maniola jurtina

SIZE AND DESCRIPTION Forewing is 20–26 mm. Brown and orange. Upper wing has a single black eye with a white highlight. Females are larger than males. The green larva has a white stripe along the side.

HABITAT Grassland; also woodland in southern Europe. Very common across Europe southwards from southern Scandinavia up to 2000 m.

FOOD/HABITS Flies May to September. Larvae feed on grasses. Winters as a larva.

Large ringlet
Erebia euryale
SIZE AND DESCRIPTION Forewing is
20–22 mm. Upperside is black-brown
with bands of orange-red on which are
small black eyespots. Underside is
slightly paler red-brown with small
eyespots. The female has more yellow
bands. Eyespots vary in size and number.
HABITAT Found from 900–1800 m.
Occurs in mountainous areas of central
Europe, such as Pyrenees, Carpathians,
Switzerland and German Alps.
FOOD/HABITS Flies in July and August.
Larvae feed on grasses.

Ringlet
Aphantopus hyperantus
SIZE AND DESCRIPTION Forewing is
20–24 mm. Upperside is very dark
brown-black, with small rather
indistinct eyespots. Underside is slightly
paler with clearer eyespots ringed with
yellow. Female is slightly paler. Larva is
pale yellow with dark band.
HABITAT Found in woodland rides and
clearings, and damp grassy areas up to
1500 m in western Europe.
FOOD/HABITS Flies in June and July.
Larvae feed on grasses. Overwinters as
caterpillar, then pupates on the ground.

Large heath
Coenonympha tullia
SIZE AND DESCRIPTION
Forewing is 19–20 mm. Upperside is a
dull grey-brown washed with orange,
forewing has small eyespots and
hindwing has several eyespots.
Underside has forewing golden brown,
hindwing slightly darker with more
obvious eyespots. Female is slightly
paler. Larva is green with dark green
line along back.
HABITAT Found in boggy areas,
mosses. Meadows from lowland
upwards. Occurs in northern and
eastern Europe.
FOOD/HABITS Flies in June and early
July. Larvae feed on cotton-grass
and sedge.

Small heath
Coenonympha pamphilius
SIZE AND DESCRIPTION Forewing
14–16 mm. Orange-brown with very
small dark "eyes". Green larva with
white stripe along the side.
HABITAT Grassy places up to 2000 m.
Across Europe except northernmost
Scandinavia.
FOOD/HABITS Flies from April to
October. Pupa feeds on grasses. 1–3
broods. Winters as larva.

Speckled wood

Pararge aegeria

SIZE AND DESCRIPTION Forewing is 19–22 mm. Yellow- or orange-and-brown wings. Orange-spotted form, *P. aegeria*, south-west Europe and Italy; cream-spotted form, *P. a. tircis*, elsewhere. Green caterpillar.

HABITAT Woodland clearings, gardens and paths across Europe from southern Scandinavia.

FOOD/HABITS Flies March to October. Feeds on grasses. Single-brooded in north. Overwinters in both larval and pupal forms.

Wall brown

Lasiommata megera

SIZE AND DESCRIPTION Forewing is 17–25 mm. Brown-and-orange patterned, with "eyes" on the forewings. Underside of hindwing is pale silvery-brown. Green caterpillar.

HABITAT Rough grassy places and gardens. British Isles (not northern Scotland) and across from southern Europe.

FOOD/HABITS Flies March to October. Adults sunbathe on walls and fences. Food plants are grasses. Two or three broods. Overwinters as a larva.

Dingy skipper
Erynnis tages
SIZE AND DESCRIPTION Forewing is 13–14 mm. Upperside is brown with tiny white spots near margin of forewing and hindwing. Underside is paler. Female is similar. Larva is green with dark green line down back, and black head.
HABITAT Usually found on banks of wildflowers on lime-soils up to 1800 m. Occurs in southern and central Europe including England, Wales and southern Scandinavia.
FOOD/HABITS Flies in May and June. Larvae feed on bird's-foot trefoil, scorpion vetch and other vetches.

Small skipper
Thymelicus flavus
SIZE AND DESCRIPTION Forewing is 13–15 mm. Bright orange wings. The body is stout and rather moth-like. Tends to hold its wings flat when at rest.
HABITAT Grassy places. England, Wales and mainland Europe south from Denmark.
FOOD/HABITS Flies May to August. Swift, darting flight. The small green larvae feed briefly on grasses, but go into hibernation almost immediately after hatching.

Large skipper
Ochlodes venatus
SIZE AND DESCRIPTION Forewing is 14–17 mm. Upperside is
orange-brown with dark veins and dark margins. Underside
paler with similar markings. Larva is blue-green with dark line
along back and yellow line down side.
HABITAT Lives in meadows and grassy banks, woodland edges,
up to 1800 m. Occurs throughout Europe including England
and Wales (absent Ireland) and southern Scandinavia.
FOOD/HABITS Flies in June to August. Larvae feed on grasses
such as cock's-foot. Overwinters as caterpillar.

Tapestry moth
Trichophaga tapetzella
SIZE AND DESCRIPTION
Forewing is 8–10 mm.
Greyish-white wings have
brown patches towards
the thorax.

HABITAT Found in stables and
buildings with high humidity.

FOOD/HABITS Flies in June and July. The
tapestry is a clothes moth whose
larvae feed on animal fibres such as
wool. Found in horsehair stuffing and
owl pellets.

Leaf-mining moth
Stigmella aurella

SIZE AND DESCRIPTION Forewing is
3 mm. The forewings have yellow
bars and purplish wingtips. Pale,
feathery underwings. The tiny leaf-
mining larva creates pale, squiggly lines
on bramble leaves.

HABITAT Woodland, hedges and
gardens over most of Europe, except
the far north.

FOOD/HABITS Flies May to September.
The food plant is bramble. Larvae
overwinter in the leaf-mines, but leave
before pupating.

Lampronia rubiella

SIZE AND DESCRIPTION Forewing is 5 mm. Two yellow or cream bars on the dark brown wings.

HABITAT Gardens with raspberries. Found across northern and central Europe.

FOOD/HABITS Flies in May and June. Larvae feed in the central stalks of raspberry fruit in summer. They overwinter in the soil and then complete their growth in buds during spring.

Common clothes moth
Tineola biselliella

SIZE AND DESCRIPTION Forewing is 4–6 mm. Goldish forewings and silvery hindwings. The white larva has a pale brown head.

HABITAT Rarely seen outdoors. The most common and destructive clothes moth.

FOOD/HABITS Adults are found throughout the year. Rarely flies, preferring to scuttle for cover. Larvae eat animal fibres and also build shelters out of them.

Green oak tortrix moth
Tortrix viridana

SIZE AND DESCRIPTION Forewing is about 10 mm. Pale green forewings and pale grey hindwings. Green larva measures about 12 mm long.

HABITAT Woods, parks and gardens with oaks.

FOOD/HABITS Flies May to August at night, but lives for only one week. The larvae feed on the buds and rolled leaves of oak trees. Will hang on a thread from trees.

Codlin moth
Cydia pomonella

SIZE AND DESCRIPTION Forewing is about 7–10 mm. Grey
forewing has black and yellowish marks towards the tips. White
larva has a brown head, becoming pinkish as it grows larger.
HABITAT Orchards, parks, gardens and hedges with apple trees.
All Europe, except the far north.
FOOD/HABITS Flies May to October. Two broods. Larvae bore
into apples (and pears) to eat both the flesh and developing
seeds. Pupates under loose bark in a cocoon, from which it
emerges during spring.

Small magpie
Eurrhypara hortulata
SIZE AND DESCRIPTION
Forewing is about 15
mm. Silky white, with
dark grey markings and
a yellowish-gold thorax
with black spots. Green
caterpillar.
HABITAT Hedgerows, woodland
margins and waste ground with
nettles. All Europe, except the far north.
FOOD/HABITS Flies June to August. Larvae feed
on stinging nettles and related plants. Winters
as a larva in a spun cocoon among plant debris.

Gold fringe
Hypsopygia costalis
SIZE AND DESCRIPTION Forewing is
8 mm. The dark brown forewings
have two gold marks and a golden
yellow fringe. The hindwings are
purplish with a gold fringe. Larva
is whitish with a brown head.
HABITAT Hedges around grassy places
in southern Britain and south/central
Europe.
FOOD/HABITS Flies July to October.
Larvae feed on dead grasses and thatch.

White plume
Pterophorus pentadactyla
SIZE AND DESCRIPTION Forewing is 12–15 mm. White, with each forewing being split into two feathery sections and each hindwing into three feathery sections. The bright green larva has tufts of silvery hair.
HABITAT Hedgerows, waste ground and gardens across Europe.
FOOD/HABITS Flies May to August at night. Larvae feed on bindweeds, curled up in a leaf. Overwinters as a small caterpillar.

Ghost swift
Hepialus humuli
SIZE AND DESCRIPTION
Forewing is 21 mm.
Male is very pale, creamy white. Female is a little larger and darker. Larva is also very pale white to grey-white with dark spots and red-brown head.
HABITAT Found in downland, meadows and gardens. Widespread throughout northern and central Europe including Great Britain.
FOOD/HABITS Flies in June. Eggs laid in flight. Larvae feed on grasses and herbaceous plants, feeding below ground on roots. May take two years to reach pupation stage, which occurs in May.

Common swift
Hepialus lupulinus

SIZE AND DESCRIPTION Forewing is 12–18 mm. Brown wings with white marks. Very short antennae. Wings are held tightly to the body when at rest. White or creamy larva is about 35 mm long with a brown head.

HABITAT Arable land, gardens, parks and grassland over most of Europe, except Iberia.

FOOD/HABITS Flies May to August at dusk. The caterpillar lives in soil, eating the roots of grasses and other herbaceous plants. Overwinters as a caterpillar.

Leopard moth
Zeuzera pyrina
SIZE AND DESCRIPTION Forewing is 20–35 mm. White, with finely spotted wings and six black marks on its furry thorax. The abdomen is ringed with greyish black. Females are much larger than males. The creamy larva has black spots and a dark head.
HABITAT Woods, parks, orchards and gardens. Found across central and southern Europe from England.
FOOD/HABITS Flies June to August at night. Single-brooded. Larvae tunnel into broad-leaved trees and shrubs.

Goat moth
Cossus cossus
SIZE AND DESCRIPTION Forewing is about 30 mm. Greyish-brown wings with fine dark patterning on forewings. The abdomen is distinctly ringed. Large and solid-looking. The purplish-red larva emits a goat-like smell.
HABITAT Broad-leaved woodland from Ireland and England south across Europe.
FOOD/HABITS Flies June to August. The larvae feed on the solid wood of broad-leaved trees for about three years before pupating in the ground.

Forester
Adscita statices
SIZE AND DESCRIPTION Forewing is 13 mm. Upperside forewing is metallic green. Larva is dull yellow with tiny black spots and small tufts.
HABITAT Found in chalk downland, sea cliffs, meadows and heaths. Occurs widely throughout Europe.
FOOD/HABITS This moth flies by day during June. One generation a year. Larvae feed on sorrel. Hibernates as caterpillar.

Five-spot burnet
Zygaena trifolii

SIZE AND DESCRIPTION Forewing is 16 mm. Upperside has metallic green forewings with five crimson spots. Hindwing is crimson, bordered green. Larva is very like that of six-spot burnet, but more blue-green.

HABITAT Found in chalk downland, meadows and marshy ground. Widespread in Europe but in Great Britain, mainly in southern England and parts of Wales.

FOOD/HABITS Flies in May to July. One generation a year. Larvae feed on bird's-foot trefoil. Overwinters as caterpillar. May take two years to pupate.

Six-spot burnet
Zygaena filipendulae

SIZE AND DESCRIPTION Forewing is 16–20 mm. Upperside has very dark metallic green-black forewing with six crimson spots; hindwing is crimson, bordered green. Larva is greenish yellow with two lines of large black spots along back.

HABITAT Found in meadows, downland, sea cliffs and woodland. Occurs widely throughout Europe and Great Britain but more coastal in Scotland.

FOOD/HABITS Flies in June and July. Larvae feed on bird's-foot trefoil and other vetches. Overwinters as caterpillar. May take two years to reach maturity.

Currant clearwing
Synanthedon tipuliformis
SIZE AND DESCRIPTION Forewing is about
8 mm. Wings are largely transparent.
Black abdomen has four yellow rings in
the male and three in the female. The
dingy white larva has a brown head and
yellow spots. The currant clearwing
usually rests with its wings apart.
HABITAT Woods, gardens and open
country with suitable foodplants
across Europe.
FOOD/HABITS Flies May to July. Single-
brooded. Larvae feed inside the stems
of blackcurrant, whitecurrant and
gooseberry. Winters as a larva.

Large red-belted clearwing
Synanthedon culiciformis
SIZE AND DESCRIPTION Forewing is
11–14 mm. The red belt refers to a
band on the abdomen. Wings are
bordered black.
HABITAT Found in open woodland,
heathland. Common and widespread in
Europe (but not in Ireland).
FOOD/HABITS Flies in May and June.
Larvae feed on birch under the bark of
stumps, sometimes in alder, where it
pupates. Overwinters as pupa. One
generation a year.

Oak eggar
Lasiocampa quercus
Size and description
Forewing is 29–45 mm. Upperside chocolate-brown, both fore
and hindwings, outer third paler. Small dark-ringed white spot
on forewing. Female considerably larger, paler with dark-ringed
white spot on forewing. Larva is hairy, dark brown, with
black rings.
Habitat Found in woodland, hedgerows, also heathland
and moors. Occurs throughout Europe and widespread in
British Isles.
Food/habits Flies in May and June. Larvae feed on wide range
of plants depending on subspecies, including oak, heather and
bramble. Overwinters as caterpillar.

Lackey moth
Malacosoma neustria
SIZE AND DESCRIPTION
Forewing is 13–20 mm.
Comes in a range of browns.
Similar to the fox moth, but
wing bands curve inwards.
Long, tufted, grey-blue larva has
white, orange, black and yellow
stripes along its body.
HABITAT Many habitats over most of
Europe, except Scotland and northern Scandinavia.
FOOD/HABITS Flies June to August at night. Single-
brooded. Larvae live in colonies in cocoons, feeding
on the leaves of hawthorn, blackthorn, plums and
sallows. Winters as an egg.

Fox moth
Macrothylacia rubi
SIZE AND DESCRIPTION Forewing is
20–30 mm. Males are fox-coloured, with
two narrow pale strips on the forewings;
females are paler. The larva is velvety and
very dark brown, with orange bands.
HABITAT Heathland, moorland, open
countryside and woodland margins.
FOOD/HABITS Flies May to July. The male flies in
sunshine and at night, the female is a purely
nocturnal flier. Larvae feed on bramble, heather,
bilberry and creeping willow. Overwinters as a
full-grown larva.

Drinker
Philudoria potatoria
SIZE AND DESCRIPTION Forewing is 25–35 mm. Male's upperwing
orange-brown with two dark lines and two white spots. Female
is slightly larger, similar wing markings but yellow-orange
ground colour. Antennae are very feathery. Larva is hairy, blue-
grey with black sides.
HABITAT Found in open woodland, damp moors and fens.
Occurs widely throughout Europe and British Isles.
FOOD/HABITS Flies in July. One generation a year. Larvae feed
on grasses such as cock's-foot and couch grass. Overwinters
as caterpillar.

Emperor moth
Saturnia pavonia

SIZE AND DESCRIPTION Forewing is 34–42 mm. Large moth with single big startling eyespots on both fore and hindwings. Female is larger and paler than male. Larva is green, banded black, with tufts.

HABITATS Found in moors, heaths, mountainsides and woodland. Occurs widely throughout Europe and British Isles.

FOOD/HABITS Flies in spring, laying eggs in May. Larvae feed principally on heather but also a range of other plants including bramble, blackthorn, hawthorn and bilberry. Overwinters as pupa.

Kentish glory
Endromis versicolora
SIZE AND DESCRIPTION Forewing is 28–36 mm. Upperside forewing buffy brown with white and black markings. Hindwings is more yellow. Female is larger and paler than male. Larva is large and green with whitish oblique stripes and hump on rear of body.
HABITAT Found in woodland and moorland with woods. Widespread throughout Europe but localised in British Isles. Occurs in northern Scotland.
FOOD/HABITS Flies in April. Larvae feed mainly on silver birch and sometimes on alder. Overwinters as pupa.

Lappet moth
Gastropacha quercifolia
SIZE AND DESCRIPTION Forewing is about 30 mm. Females are much larger than males. Varies across its range, from purple in the north to pale brown in south. At rest, the wings resemble dead leaves. Larva is dark brownish-grey, with two bluish bands near its head.
HABITAT Open woodland, hedges, orchards and gardens.
FOOD/HABITS Flies May to August at night. Single-brooded. Larvae feed on blackthorn, buckthorn, apples and sallows. Overwinters as a larva.

Peach blossom
Thyatira batis

SIZE AND DESCRIPTION Forewing is about 15 mm. Forewings are
brown with pink blotches. The larva is dark brown, with
slanting white lines and bumps on its back.

HABITAT Woodland and woodland edges in northern and
central Europe, including the British Isles.

FOOD/HABITS Flies May to August at night. Single-brooded.
Larvae feed on bramble, raspberry and blackberry.
Overwinters as a pupa.

Large emerald
Geometra papilionaria

SIZE AND DESCRIPTION Forewing is 25–32 mm. Upperside is pale blue-green marked with faint white lines and spots. Sexes are similar but shade of green and number of markings may vary. Larva is rough-skinned, body coloured yellowish green with reddish warts on back.

HABITAT Found in woodland, moors and heathland, and fens. Occurs widely in central and northern Europe including British Isles.

FOOD/HABITS Flies in July. Larvae feed on trees such as silver birch, alder, beech and hazel. Overwinters as caterpillar.

Winter moth
Operophtera brumata
SIZE AND DESCRIPTION Forewing is about 15 mm. Males have greyish-brown, faintly patterned wings; females have stunted, relict wings. The green looper caterpillar is about 20 mm long.
HABITAT Abundant wherever there are trees and shrubs.
FOOD/HABITS Flies October to February. Nocturnal and attracted to lighted windows. Females can be seen on windowsills and tree-trunks. Larvae feed on deciduous trees. A serious pest of hard fruits, especially apples.

Garden carpet
Xanthorhoe fluctuata
SIZE AND DESCRIPTION Forewing is about 14 mm. Greyish-white wings, with markings in various shades of grey. Pattern varies, but there is always a dark triangle where forewings join thorax. Larva is a twig-like looper whose colour ranges from grey-green to dark brown.
HABITAT Common in cultivated areas.

FOOD/HABITS Flies April to October from dusk. Rests on walls and fences during the day. Two or three broods. Larvae feed on perennial wall-rocket, garlic mustard and other crucifers. Winters as a pupa.

Small emerald
Hemistola chrysoprasaria
SIZE AND DESCRIPTION Forewing is 18 mm. Pale grey-green, with two fine white lines on the forewing and a single line on the hindwing. The larva is pale green, with white dots and a brown head.
HABITAT Downland, hedges and woodland edges, usually on chalk or limestone.
FOOD/HABITS Flies May to August at night. Single-brooded. Larvae feed on traveller's joy.

Brimstone
Opisthograptis luteolata
SIZE AND DESCRIPTION Forewing is
15–20 mm. Sulphur yellow, with brown
flecks on leading edge of forewing.
Brown looper caterpillar is about 30
mm long, often tinged grey or green,
with a prominent nodule on the middle
of its back.
HABITAT Woods, hedges and gardens.
FOOD/HABITS Flies April to October at
night. Caterpillar feeds on hawthorn,
blackthorn and other shrubs.

Lime-speck pug
Eupithecia centaurearia
SIZE AND DESCRIPTION Forewing is
about 12 mm. Pale grey, with dark
marks on the forewings. The green or
yellow larva often has red spots.
HABITAT Rough areas and gardens.
FOOD/HABITS Flies May to October
from dusk. Rests with its wings
outstretched on lichens on walls and
tree-trunks. May be double-brooded.
Larvae feed on a range of herbaceous
plants, such as yarrow and ragwort.
Overwinters as a pupa.

Magpie moth
Abraxas grossulariata
SIZE AND DESCRIPTION Forewing is about 20 mm. Variable black-and-white pattern, with a yellowish-orange line across the middle of the forewing and near the head. The larva, about 30 mm long, is pale green with black spots and a rusty line along its sides. Caterpillar is a looper, black spots on white body with reddish sides.

HABITAT Woods, gardens and hedges.

FOOD/HABITS Flies June to August. Larvae feed on blackthorn, currants, hawthorn, gooseberry and many other shrubs. Overwinters as a small caterpillar and pupates in May or June.

August thorn
Ennomos quercinaria
SIZE AND DESCRIPTION Forewing is
about 17 mm. Pale yellowish-tan,
with two narrow brown stripes
on each forewing. Abdomen is
fluffy. The greyish-brown looper
caterpillar has nodules that make it
look like a twig.
HABITAT Woodland, parks and
gardens. Locally common south
from Scotland.
FOOD/HABITS Flies August and September at
night. Larvae feed on oaks and other trees.

Large thorn
Ennomos autumnaria
SIZE AND DESCRIPTION Forewing
is 12–25 mm. Upperside varies
from pale to deep yellow with
purplish-brown speckling. Larva
looks like a little twig. It is very
slender, coloured brown or
greenish brown.
HABITAT Found in woodland
and bushy areas. Occurs widely
throughout Europe.
FOOD/HABITS Flies in September. Larvae feed on trees
such as silver birch, alder, hawthorn and blackthorn.
Overwinters as egg which hatches in spring.

Swallowtailed moth
Ourapteryx sambucaria
SIZE AND DESCRIPTION
Forewing is 25–30 mm.
Wings are bright lemon,
rapidly fading to pale
cream or white. Caterpillar
is a brown looper and up
to 50 mm long.
HABITAT Forest edges,
woods, gardens, scrub and
parks across Europe, except
the far north.

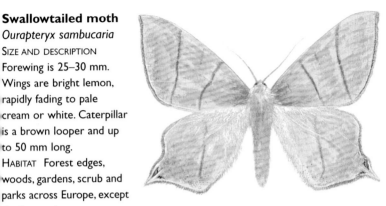

FOOD/HABITS Flies June to August at night, often coming
to lighted windows. Larvae feed on blackthorn,
hawthorn, ivy and numerous other trees and bushes.

Mottled umber
Erannis defoliaria
SIZE AND DESCRIPTION Forewing is
20–22 mm. Upperside creamy brown,
forewing with darker bands, hindwing pale
and speckled. Female is wingless and clings
to trunks and stems of foodplants. Larva is
dark olive-green with greenish-yellow
broken stripe along side.
HABITATS Found in woodland throughout
Europe including England and Wales, rare in
Scotland and Ireland.

FOOD/HABITS Flies in October. Larvae feed on a variety
of trees, especially birch, oak, hornbeam, blackthorn and
hawthorn. Overwinters as egg, which hatches in spring.

Peppered moth
Biston betularia

SIZE AND DESCRIPTION Forewing is 20–30 mm. Variable. Normal form is white, peppered with fine dark marks, or sooty black. The green or brown looper caterpillar is up to 60 mm long.

HABITAT Woods, gardens, scrub and parks across Europe, except the far north.

FOOD/HABITS Flies May to August, coming to lighted windows. Larvae feed on a range of trees and shrubs, including sallow, hawthorn, golden rod and raspberry.

Death's head hawkmoth
Acherontia atropos
SIZE AND DESCRIPTION Forewing is 50–67 mm. Upperside with
mottled forewing and pale orange hindwing with two dark
bands. Skull-like markings on thorax make this large moth
unmistakable. Larva is variable coloured – may be yellow green
or brown with dark diagonal stripes.
HABITAT Found in gardens and fields. Migratory to Europe
including occasionally to southern England.
FOOD/HABITS May breed successfully in Europe, but rarely in
British Isles. Larvae feed on potato plants and similar.

Privet hawkmoth
Sphinx ligustri

SIZE AND DESCRIPTION Forewing is up to 55 mm. Brown wings have black markings. There is a tan trailing edge to the forewing. The body is striped with pink and black. Green caterpillar has seven purple-and-white stripes on each side of its body.

HABITAT Woodland edges, hedges, parks and gardens across Europe, except Ireland, Scotland and the far north of Scandinavia.

FOOD/HABITS Flies June to July, drinking nectar on the wing, especially from honeysuckle. Larvae feed on privet, ash and lilac. Overwinters as a pupa in the soil.

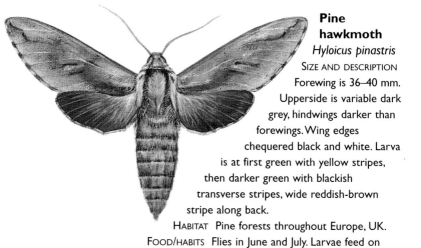

Pine hawkmoth
Hyloicus pinastris
SIZE AND DESCRIPTION
Forewing is 36–40 mm.
Upperside is variable dark
grey, hindwings darker than
forewings. Wing edges
chequered black and white. Larva
is at first green with yellow stripes,
then darker green with blackish
transverse stripes, wide reddish-brown
stripe along back.
HABITAT Pine forests throughout Europe, UK.
FOOD/HABITS Flies in June and July. Larvae feed on
Scots pine and Norway spruce. Overwinters as pupa.

Poplar hawkmoth
Laothoe populi
SIZE AND DESCRIPTION
Forewing 40 mm.
Variable colouring, from
grey to pinkish-brown.
Orange patches on hindwings.
At rest, gives the impression of
a bunch of dead leaves. The green
caterpillar, up to 60 mm long, has a
yellow horn and seven diagonal yellow stripes.
HABITAT Woodland margins, river valleys and parks
throughout Europe, except the far north.
FOOD/HABITS A slow-flying moth that is on the wing between
May and September. Its larvae feed on poplars and sallows.

Eyed hawkmoth
Smerinthus ocellatus

SIZE AND DESCRIPTION Forewing is up to 45 mm. There is a wavy trailing edge to the forewing; the hindwing is pink, with a large blue "eye". The bright green caterpillar has seven diagonal yellow stripes on each side of its body and a greenish-blue horn at the rear.

HABITAT Open woodland, parks and gardens across Europe, but not Scotland or northern Scandinavia.

FOOD/HABITS Flies May to July. Comes towards light. Larvae feed on willows and apples. Overwinters as a pupa in the soil.

Striped hawkmoth
Hyles lineata
SIZE AND DESCRIPTION
Forewing is 39–45 mm.
Upperside has dark olive-
brown forewings with white
stripes and pink hindwings bordered
with black. Larva is dark green or black
with small yellow spots.
HABITAT Found in gardens and hedgerows,
worldwide.
FOOD/HABITS Flies in May to October. Larvae
feed on snapdragon and hedge bedstraw.
Overwinters as a pupa. One generation a year.

Hummingbird hawkmoth
Macroglossum stellatarum
SIZE AND DESCRIPTION Forewing is
about 25 mm. Mousey-grey forewings
and a hairy thorax. Hindwings are golden
orange. The caterpillar, about 50 mm long,
is green with yellow, white and green
horizontal stripes.
HABITAT Parks, gardens and flowery banks.
Found in southern Europe, moving northwards
in summer, reaching Britain in varying numbers.
FOOD/HABITS Day-flying throughout the year.
Usually seen in summer in Britain. Hovers in
front of flowers, drinking nectar through its
long proboscis. Caterpillars feed on bedstraws.

Elephant hawkmoth
Deilephila elpenor

SIZE AND DESCRIPTION Forewing is 31–36 mm. Upperside has olive-brown forewings, pink and brown hindwings. Larva is large, yellowish or green, with conspicuous large eye spots on segments 2 and 3, which it uses in defence display.

HABITAT Found in woodland clearings, meadows, gardens, river valleys and waste ground. Occurs widely in Europe.

FOOD/HABITS Flies in June. Larvae feed on willowherb, bedstraw, bogbean, fuchsia and evening primrose. Overwinters as pupa.

Buff-tip
Phalera bucephala

SIZE AND DESCRIPTION
Forewing is up to 30
mm. Silver-grey wings,
with an orange tip to
each forewing and an
orange head, giving a
broken-twig appearance when
at rest. The caterpillar is
about 45 mm long, with
yellow stripes and sparse hairs.

HABITAT Woods, parks, orchards and gardens
throughout Europe.

FOOD/HABITS Flies May to August. Caterpillars feed
on leaves of oaks, limes, elms and other trees.

Great prominant
Peridea anceps

SIZE AND DESCRIPTION
Forewing is 26–36
mm. Forewings greyish
brown with darker
markings of grey, red-
brown and ochre. Hindwings
are yellowish white. Females
are slightly larger than males.
There is a melanic form. Larva is
yellow-green with yellow and reddish oblique stripes on sides.

HABITAT Widely distributed and moderately common in Europe, except
for extreme north. Not found in northern Scotland nor in Ireland.

FOOD/HABITS Flies in April to June. Larvae feed on oak. Overwinters as
pupa. Single generation a year.

Pussmoth
Cerura vinula

SIZE AND DESCRIPTION Forewing is 31–40 mm. Uppersides with white forewings intricately patterned with black. Hindwings are greyish with dark veins. Larva is stout, bright green, with black diamond-shaped saddle, two long tails at rear and brown head surrounded by pink.

HABITAT Found in woods and hedges, throughout Europe. Widespread in the British Isles.

FOOD/HABITS Flies in May and June. Larvae feed on trees such as willow, sallow, aspen and poplar. Overwinters as pupa.

Figure-of-eight
Diloba caeruleocephala
SIZE AND DESCRIPTION   Forewing is about 15 mm. Brown-and-grey forewing has a figure-of-eight marking. Hindwing is pale grey-brown. The grey-blue caterpillar has black spots and yellow lines.
HABITAT   Woodlands, scrub and gardens across Europe.
FOOD/HABITS   Flies September to October. Larvae feed on hawthorn, blackthorn and other rosaceous shrubs.

Vapourer
Orgyia antiqua
SIZE AND DESCRIPTION   Forewing is 15–18 mm. Chestnut, with a white spot on each forewing. Male is winged, but the female has only vestigial wings. Caterpillar is dark grey, with red spots and four cream tufts of hair on the back. Its body is covered with finer hairs.
HABITAT   Woods, parks, gardens, hedges and tree-lined streets across Europe.
FOOD/HABITS   Flies June to October, the males by day, the females at night. Caterpillars feed on a range of deciduous trees. Eggs overwinter.

Brown-tail
Euproctis chrysorrhoea
SIZE AND DESCRIPTION Forewing is up to 20 mm. Totally white and rather hairy. Males have brown abdomens. Females have white abdomens with brown tufts at the end. Caterpillar is black with a white stripe and yellow tufts of hair, which can cause rashes if touched.
HABITAT Woods, hedges, parks and gardens from eastern and southern England across much of mainland Europe.
FOOD/HABITS Flies July to August. Caterpillars feed in groups on many species of tree and bush.

Yellow-tail
Euproctis similis
SIZE AND DESCRIPTION Forewing is up to 20 mm. Totally white and rather hairy. Males have thinner abdomens than females; both sexes have yellow tufts at the end. The black caterpillar is up to 40 mm long, with red stripes and white spots. It is very hairy, and contact with skin can cause a rash.
HABITAT Woods, gardens, parks, orchards, tree-lined streets and hedges. Most of Europe, but rare in Scotland and Ireland.
FOOD/HABITS Flies June to August. Larvae feed on hawthorn, blackthorn and fruit trees.

Gypsy moth
Lymantria dispar
SIZE AND DESCRIPTION Forewing is 24–32 mm. Male is dark dusky brown, female mainly white. Female does not fly. Larva is pale yellowish, with dark grey stripes and tufts of hairs.
HABITAT Occurs in woodland, widespread throughout Europe but no longer in British Isles except as an occasional migrant.
FOOD/HABITS Flies in July and August. Overwinters as egg, to hatch the following spring. Young larvae are dispersed on the wind. Larvae feed on trees, especially oak and poplar.

Common footman
Eilema lurideola
SIZE AND DESCRIPTION Forewing is about 15 mm. Pale grey forewing is fringed with yellow. Hindwings are pale yellow. Rests with nearly flat wings. The hairy grey larva has black lines on its back and red lines on its sides.
HABITAT Hedges, woods and orchards across Europe.
FOOD/HABITS Flies June to August. Larvae eat lichen.

Garden tiger
Arctia caja

SIZE AND DESCRIPTION Forewing is 25–35 mm. Chocolate-brown forewing has cream patterning. Hindwings are orange with black spots. The very hairy black-and-brown caterpillar is known as a "woolly bear".

HABITAT Open habitats, including gardens and scrub throughout Europe.

FOOD/HABITS Flies June to August. Caterpillar feeds on herbaceous plants. Winters as a small caterpillar.

Jersey tiger

Euplagia quadripunctaria

SIZE AND DESCRIPTION
Forewing is 26–32 mm.
Uppersides has pied forewing
chocolate-brown and creamy
white, bright orange hindwing
with chocolate-brown blotchy
spots. Thorax brown with yellow
sides, abdomen bright orange. Larva is
dark brown with tufts of paler hairs.

HABITAT Found in open countryside and mountain slopes and
valleys. Widespread in central and southern Europe. In England
restricted to the south-west.

FOOD/HABITS Flies in August. Larvae feed on variety of plants such
as dandelion. Overwinters as caterpillar. Single generation a year.

White ermine

Spilosoma lubricipeda

SIZE AND DESCRIPTION Forewing
is 15–20 mm. White, with more
or less sparse black spots. Hairy
thorax and yellow, black-spotted
abdomen. The larva is up to 45
mm long, dark brown and very hairy,
with a dark red line down its back.

HABITAT Hedgerows, gardens, waste ground and
other habitats throughout Europe.

FOOD/HABITS Flies May to August. Adults do not
feed, but larvae feed on herbaceous plants, including
docks, dandelions and numerous garden plants.

Buff ermine
Spilosoma lutea

SIZE AND DESCRIPTION Forewing is 17–20 mm. Pale buff to creamy yellow, with a variable broken dark line on the forewing. The larva is up to 45 mm long and has tufts of long brown hairs.

HABITAT Most habitats, but especially common on waste ground and in gardens throughout Europe.

FOOD/HABITS Flies May to August. Larvae feed on wild and garden herbaceous plants.

Cinnibar
Tyria jacobaeae
SIZE AND DESCRIPTION Forewing is 15–20 mm. Upperside with very dark greyish black forewing with scarlet streaks and spots; hindwing is scarlet. Larva is slender, banded black and yellow.
HABITAT Found in waste ground, newly disturbed ground, roadsides, meadows, heathland. Widespread throughout Europe.
FOOD/HABITS Flies in May to July. Night-flying but easily disturbed from daytime resting place in low herbage. Larvae feed on species of ragwort and groundsel. The larvae feed in groups. Single generation a year. Overwinters as pupa.

Pine processionary
Thaumetopoea pitycampa
SIZE AND DESCRIPTION Forewing is 20–25 mm. Uppersides with
greyish white forewings with dark brown leading edge and
broken dark margin and dark bands. Hindwing pale with single
black spot on rear edge. Larva is grey-black with white hairs
and red-brown warts, extremely irritating to skin if touched.
HABITAT Found in forests in Mediterranean Europe.
FOOD/HABITS Larvae feed on pine needles. They live
communally in large silken tents nestled among pine twigs.
Caterpillars move in single file in a long line to new feeding
sites. A serious forest pest.

Garden dart
Euxoa nigricans
SIZE AND DESCRIPTION Forewing is
16–20 mm. Upperwing with grey-
brown forewing, pale whitish hindwing.
Larva is ochreous brown with
short hairs.
HABITAT Found in farmland, gardens, marshy
areas, commons and waste ground. Occurs
widely throughout Europe.
FOOD/HABITS Flies in July and August. Larvae
feed on wide variety of plants such as plantain,
clover, dock and hogweed, as well as lettuce.
Overwinters as egg. One generation a year.

Heart and dart
Agrotis exclamationis
SIZE AND DESCRIPTION
Forewing is about 20 mm.
Background colour varies from
greyish-brown to deep brown.
Wings have vaguely heart-shaped
and dart-shaped markings. The larva,
about 40 mm long, is a dull brown and
grey "cutworm".
HABITAT Almost any habitat, especially cultivated.
Found throughout Europe.
FOOD/HABITS Flies May to September at night. The
larvae feed on the stems of herbaceous plants at
night and hide in soil during the daytime.

Large yellow underwing
Noctua pronuba

SIZE AND DESCRIPTION Forewing is 25 mm. Varies from pale to dark brown. The hindwings are deep yellow with a black border. The yellow flashes when the moth takes flight, which is thought to confuse predators. The green larva, up to 50 mm long, has two rows of dark markings on its back.

HABITAT Well-vegetated habitats across Europe, except in the far north.

FOOD/HABITS Flies June to October. Flight is fast and erratic. The yellow flashes shown in flight become invisible the moment it lands.

Chinese character
Cilix glaucata

SIZE AND DESCRIPTION Forewing is 14–16 mm. Uppersides white, forewing bordered grey with spots near outer edge and broad mark. Hindwing with grey outer border. Larva is reddish-brown with black lines.

HABITAT Found in woodland edges, hedgerows. Widespread in central and southern Europe.

FOOD/HABITS Flies in May and June and again in July and August. Larvae feed on blackthorn, hawthorn, and fruit trees such as plum and pear. Two generations a year. Overwinters as pupa.

Setaceous hebrew character
Xestia c-nigrum

SIZE AND DESCRIPTION Forewing is up to 20 mm. Greyish-brown to chestnut with a purplish tinge. There is a pale patch on the leading edge of the forewing. The larva is initially green, before becoming pale greenish-grey.

HABITAT Almost anywhere in Europe, except in the far north.

FOOD/HABITS Flies May to October, when it is at its commonest. The larvae have a diet of herbaceous plants. Passes the winter either in the larval stage or as a pupa.

Cabbage moth
Mamestra brassicae
SIZE AND DESCRIPTION
Forewing is 15–20 mm.
Mottled greyish-brown, with
rusty scales. The plump larva,
up to 50 mm long, is brownish-
green, with rather subtle dark and
pale markings.
HABITAT Almost any habitat, but most
common on cultivated land throughout
Europe, except in the far north.
FOOD/HABITS Flies throughout the year, but
mainly between May and September. The
larvae feed on cabbages and other
herbaceous plants. Winters as a pupa.

Mouse moth
Amphipyra tragopoginis
SIZE AND DESCRIPTION Forewing is
15 mm. Dark brown, with three
dark spots. Underwings are pale.
Holds wings flat along its abdomen
when at rest. The larva is green, with
narrow white lines.

HABITAT Widespread in woods, hedgerows, gardens
and open countryside with scrub throughout Europe.
FOOD/HABITS Flies June to September. Roosts by day
in outbuildings, under loose bark and in hollow trees.
If disturbed, it scuttles off in a mouse-like fashion.
From April to June, larvae feed on plants such as salad
burnet, hawthorn and fennel.

Green arches
Anaplectoides prasina
SIZE AND DESCRIPTION
Forewing is about
20 mm. Greenish forewings
have variable black markings,
while the hindwings are dark
grey or brown. The larva is
brown with darker markings.
HABITAT Deciduous woodland over
most of Europe.
FOOD/HABITS Flies mid-June to mid-July at
night. The larvae feed on a range of plants,
especially honeysuckle and bilberry.

Clay
Mythimna ferrago
SIZE AND DESCRIPTION
Forewing is 15 mm. Colour
varies from straw to
reddish-brown, with a white
mark in the middle of the
forewing. Wings lie flat when at
rest. The pale brown larva is marked
with thin yellow lines.
HABITAT Common in grassy places across Europe.
FOOD/HABITS Flies May to August. Larvae feed on
grasses and other low-growing plants.

Old lady

Mormo maura

SIZE AND DESCRIPTION Forewing is 30–35 mm. Patterned dark brown and black, resembling an old lady's shawl. The greyish-brown larva, up to 75 mm long, has dark smudgy diamonds and a broken white line running down its back.

HABITAT Woods, hedges, gardens, parks and damp places in southern, central and western Europe. Rare in Ireland and Scotland.

FOOD/HABITS Flies July and August, often coming towards light. Larvae feed on a variety of trees and shrubs. Hibernates as a small larva.

Common wainscot
Mythimna pallens

SIZE AND DESCRIPTION Forewing is 14–16 mm. Pale-coloured moth with creamy forewing and white hindwing. Larva is ochreous with three white lines.

HABITAT Found in grassland, including meadows and marshes. Occurs widely throughout Europe, including the British Isles.

FOOD/HABITS Flies in June to October. Larvae feed on grasses such as cock's-foot and couch grass. Has two generations a year. Overwinters as caterpillar.

Burnished brass
Diachrisia chrysitis

SIZE AND DESCRIPTION Forewing is up to 20 mm. The two metallic marks on the forewings vary from emerald to deep gold. Wings are held above the abdomen when at rest. There is a prominent tuft on the thorax. The larva, up to 35 mm long, is bluish-green, with diagonal white streaks across the back and a white line along the side.

HABITAT Gardens, parks, hedges and waste ground throughout Europe.

FOOD/HABITS Flies May to October. Larvae feed on nettles and mint. Hibernates over winter in its larval form.

Mullein

Cucullia verbasci

SIZE AND DESCRIPTION Forewing is 20–25 mm. Colour varies
from pale straw to mid-brown and is darker streaked. With the
wings held close to its body, the resting moth resembles a twig.
The larva, up to 60 mm long, is creamy white and has yellow
and black spots.

HABITAT Woodland edges, scrub, river banks, gardens and parks
over most of Europe, but not Scotland, Ireland and northern
Scandinavia.

FOOD/HABITS Flies April to June. In June and July, the larvae feed
on mulleins, figworts and buddleia. The mullein overwinters
as a pupa.

Merville-du-jour
Dichonia aprilina
SIZE AND DESCRIPTION Forewing is 21–25 mm. Upperside has forewing finely patterned with white, yellow, pale green and dark brown. Hindwing greyish with dark border. Larva varies from red-brown to green-brown to grey-brown, with broken white line down centre.
HABITAT Found in parkland and oak woodland. Widespread throughout Europe but local. Widespread in Britain, more common in southern England.
FOOD/HABITS Flies in September to October. Larvae feed on oak, first on buds, then on leaves. Overwinters as egg. Single generation a year.

Grey chi
Antitype chi
SIZE AND DESCRIPTION
Forewing is 15 mm. Mottled grey wings, with a small but distinct dark cross in the middle of the forewing. The bluish-green larva has green-edged white lines along its body.

HABITAT Gardens, grassy places and moorlands in much of Europe, but not the far north.
FOOD/HABITS Flies August and September, resting on walls and rocks during the day. Larvae feed from April to early June on low plants such as dock and sorrels. Overwinters as an egg.

Angle shades
Phlogophora meticulosa
SIZE AND DESCRIPTION Forewing is about 25 mm. Varies from
brown to green, with distinctive v-shaped markings. Forewing's
trailing edge has a ragged look, exaggerated by its habit of
resting with its wings curled over. The fat, green larva, up to
45 mm long, has a white line (often faint) along its back.
HABITAT A migrant found in almost any habitat in Europe.
FOOD/HABITS Flies most of year, but mainly May to October.
Larvae feed on a variety of wild and cultivated plants.
Overwinters as a larva.

Silver Y
Autographa gamma
SIZE AND DESCRIPTION Forewing is about
20 mm. Varies from purple-tinged grey to
almost black, with a silver y-mark
on the forewing. Green larva is up to
25 mm long.
HABITAT A migrant found all over Europe.
Breeds all year in southern Europe. British and
other northern breeders do not survive winter
and are supplemented by migrants.
FOOD/HABITS Flies throughout the year. Attracted by
nectar. May be seen in autumn alongside butterflies on
buddleia. Larvae feed on low-growing wild and
cultivated plants.

Grey dagger
Acronicta psi
SIZE AND DESCRIPTION Forewing is
15–20 mm. Pale to dark grey, with
dark, apparently dagger-shaped marks.
The hairy, grey-black larva has a yellow
line along its back, red spots along its sides
and a black horn on its first abdominal segment.
HABITAT Woodlands, commons, parks and gardens
across Europe, except the far north.
FOOD/HABITS Flies May to September, with larva feeding
August to October on trees. Winters as a pupa.

Red underwing
Catocala nupta

SIZE AND DESCRIPTION Forewing is 30–35 mm. Grey mottled forewings make the moth well-camouflaged on tree-bark, but the bright red underwings are very conspicuous in flight. The pale brown caterpillar has warty, bud-like lumps on its back.

HABITAT Woodlands, hedges, gardens and parks across Europe, except northern Scandinavia.

FOOD/HABITS Flies August and September at night. Flies erratically, flashing the red underwings to confuse predators. Larvae feed from May to July on willow, poplar and aspen.

Herald
Scoliopteryx libatrix
SIZE AND DESCRIPTION Forewing is
20–25 mm. Purplish to orange
brown, with bright orange scales near
head. The trailing edge is ragged. The
slender green larva is up to 55 mm
long and has thin, pale yellow lines
along its sides.
HABITAT Woodlands, gardens, parks and
open countryside over Europe, except
northern Scandinavia.
FOOD/HABITS Flies August to October, and in spring after
migration. Larvae feed on willows and sallows. Overwinters
as an adult.

Snout
Hypena proboscidalis
SIZE AND DESCRIPTION

Forewing is 18–21 mm. Upperwing has
dark grey-brown forewing, with paler
hindwing. The long palpi (sensory organs
on the head) give this species its common
name. Larva is long and slender, yellow-green to
dark green with white lines along back and sides.
HABITAT Gardens, waste ground, open woodland,
hedgerows. Widespread in Europe including British Isles.
FOOD/HABITS Two generations. Flies in June to early
August and again in September to early October. Larvae
feed on nettle. Overwinters as caterpillar.

Addresses

Alana Ecology Ltd
The Old Primary School
Church Street
Bishop's Castle
Shropshire SY9 5AE
Tel 01588 630173
E-mail info@alanaecology.com
Website www.alanaecology.com

British Butterfly Conservation Society
Manor Yard
East Lulworth
Wareham
Dorset BH20 5QP
Tel 01929 400209
E-mail info@butterfly-conservation.org
Website www.butterfly-conservation.org

NHBS
2-3 Wills Road
Totnes
Devon TQ9 5XN
Tel 01803 865913
E-mail nhbs@nhbs.co.uk
Website www.nhbs.com

The Wildlife Trusts
The Kiln
Waterside
Mather Road
Newark
Nottinghamshire NG24 1WT
Tel 0870 036 7711
Fax 0870 036 0101
E-mail info@wildlife-trusts.cix.co.uk
Website www.wildlifetrusts.org

Wildlife Watch
(Contact details as above)
E-mail watch@wildlife-trusts.cix.co.uk

Watkins & Doncaster
PO Box 5
Cranbrook
Kent TN18 5EZ
Tel 01580 753133
Fax 01580 754054
E-mail robin.ford@virgin.net
Website www.watdon.com
(General naturalists' supplies)

Suggested reading

Ash, Jim et al
*The Millennium Atlas of Butterflies
in Britain and Ireland*
Oxford University Press, 2001

Carter, D. & Hargreaves, B.
*A Field Guide to the Caterpillars of Butterflies
and Moths in Britain and Europe*
Collins, 1986

Chinery, Michael
Butterflies of Britain and Europe
Collins and The Wildlife Trusts, 1998

Chinery, Michael
*New Generation Guide to Butterflies and
Day-flying Moths of Britain and Europe*
Collins, 1989

Chinery, Michael
*Collins Guide to the Insects of Britain
and Western Europe*
Collins, 1986

Oxford, R.
*Minibeast Magic – Kind Hearted Capture
Techniques for Invertebrates*
Yorkshire Wildlife Trust, 1999

Packham, Chris
*Chris Packham's Back Garden
Nature Reserve*
New Holland & The Wildlife Trusts, 2001

Skinner, B.
*Colour Identification Guide to Moths
of the British Isles*
Viking, 1984

Whalley, Paul
Butterflies
Mitchell Beazley, 1981

Index

Scientific names